Writing Thank-You Notes

Finding the Perfect Words

Gabrielle Goodwin & David Macfarlane

Sterling Publishing Co, Inc., New York
A Sterling/Chapelle Book

Chapelle Ltd.

Owner: Jo Packham

Editor: Linda Orton

images Copyright © 1994, 1995, 1996, 1998 Photodisc, Inc.

Staff: Marie Barber, Ann Bear, Areta Bingham, Kass Burchett, Rebecca Christensen, Holly Fuller, Marilyn Goff, Holly Hollingsworth, Shawn Hsu, Susan Jorgensen, Pauline Locke, Barbara Milburn, Karmen Quinney, Leslie Ridenour, Cindy Stoeckl

Library of Congress Cataloging-in-Publication Data

Goodwin, Gabrielle.
    Writing thank-you notes : finding the perfect words / Gabrielle
Goodwin & David Macfarlane.
        p.   cm.
    "A Sterling/Chapelle book."
    Includes index.
    ISBN 0-8069-4210-X
        1. Thank-you notes.   I. Macfarlane, David.   II. Title.
    BJ2115.T45G66   1999   98-47834
    395.4--dc21   CIP

10 9 8 7 6 5 4 3

A Sterling/Chapelle Book

Published by Sterling Publishing Company, Inc.
387 Park Avenue South, New York, NY 10016
© 1999 by Chapelle Ltd.
Distributed in Canada by Sterling Publishing
% Canadian Manda Group, One Atlantic Avenue, Suite 105
Toronto, Ontario, Canada M6K 3E7
Distributed in Great Britain and Europe by Cassell PLC
Wellington House, 125 Strand, London WC2R 0BB, England
Distributed in Australia by Capricorn Link (Australia) Pty Ltd.
P.O. Box 6651, Baulkham Hills, Business Centre, NSW 2153, Australia
Printed in the United States of America
All Rights Reserved

Sterling ISBN 0-8069-4210-X

According to legend, Gabrielle Goodwin stunned friends and family alike by sending off a brief thank-you to the doctor who brought her into the world shortly after she was born. Of course, as with most legends, this, too, may be inaccurate, in which case she will have to thank her mother, Connie Goodwin, for all that she has learned about being appropriately grateful. Viewed intermittently as vocation and avocation, Gabrielle teaches English as a Second Language in Logan, Utah, while "nursing" her husband through graduate school.

David Macfarlane, the beleaguered student, gave up a career in journalism because he likes to eat and wanted to pursue something a little less cynical—he is currently studying political science at Utah State University. For more information about making donations to this pursuit of higher knowledge, please look under www.perpetualstudent.com on the World Wide Web. Cash only, thank-you.

Table of Contents

1

Introduction

Such a sweet gift—a piece of handmade writing, in an envelope that is not a bill, sitting in our friend's path when she trudges home from a long day ... a day our words will help repair. They don't need to be immortal, just sincere. She can read them twice and again tomorrow.

Garrison Keillor

Chances are good that you, among the billions of people who inhabit this earth, are the kind of person who enjoys receiving gifts (is there any other kind?). While the odds are not as high, there is also a strong possibility that you are among the many who sweat profusely and suffer heart palpitations at the prospect of having to write a thank-you note for the aforementioned gift.

"What should I say?"

"I don't want to sound stupid!"

"I don't know the etiquette for this kind of thing."

While our primary intent here is to ease your fear of the somewhat threatening thank-you note, it is initially important to understand the significance of showing appreciation for a gift, which history bears out.

Of course, we are all almost intimately familiar with the 'feuding families' scenario which serves as the backdrop for the Shakespearean tragedy Romeo and Juliet. But unfortunately, we are left to wonder as to the cause of the acrimony between the Montagues and Capulets.

Well, it is a little known historical fact that Shakespeare penned a 'prequel' to Romeo and Juliet before his death, and in it he explained that the blood feud which separated our young lovers actually began as the result of something quite simple. As luck would have it, on the occasion of the high school graduation of the oldest Capulet child (named Hortence, I believe), the Montagues sent a very tasteful, though not ostentatious, vase accompanied by a card of congratulations. It was only one of many gifts, and unfortunately the card had been misplaced when it came time to express appreciation for the gift.

A forgivable faux pas, perhaps, but from this innocent oversight arose one of the most hostile and enduring relationships in literary history, and all the result of one little forgotten thank-you note. The source of the preceding account was Don Shakespeare, a plumber from Des Moines who is a twelfth cousin of the English bard. Disbelieve at your own peril.

Certainly, the times have changed. You will not create a war by forgetting to send a note of thanks to Aunt Emma for those barnyard place mats with matching chicken napkin rings. But words, especially those written, have the power to make a difference.

The thank-you note is an effective means for expressing feelings in a wide variety of scenarios. It is a way to celebrate and nurture relationships and is appropriate in situations other than when you receive a gift. How about a note for the man who drives your kids safely to school each day? What about the woman who cuts your hair just the way you like it every time? Would she appreciate a kind word? What about the friend who brought you dinner when you had the flu, the doorman in your apartment building, or the mechanic who gives you good service at a reasonable price—the possibilities are rather limitless.

The effectiveness of your thank-you is not determined by whether or not you can write like Shakespeare (William, not Don). You will be heard, and appreciated, if only for taking the time to write; simply express your warm feelings in your own, incomparable way. Chances are, you can even misspell a word or two and still make someone's day.

2

Why and When to Write Thank-You Notes

It pains me to think that thank-you notes may be an endangered art form. Unless some of us take the time to be vigilant about this, they may go the way of stained

Perhaps you are still a bit confused as to when a thank-you note is appropriate. The ultimate purpose of *Writing Thank-you Notes* is to offer a great deal of insight into when you should send a thank-you note.

A thank-you note is a written message to show appreciation for something someone has given you or done for you. Listed on page 10 are occasions when etiquette dictates that a thank-you must or should be written. There are an endless number of daily situations in which a thank-you note would be unexpected, but deeply appreciated. Let your conscience be your guide. Do you feel grateful? Let somebody know!

Someone has done something nice for you, whether it was giving a thoughtful gift, preparing a nice dinner, or lending a hand when you moved, and you would like to say "Thank You." Thank you for thinking of me, thank you for your help, thank you for going to such an effort, thank you for being my friend, thank you for your extravagance, thank you for making my favorite dish, thank you for entertaining me—well, you get the idea.

glass windows like those at Notre Dame and Chartres cathedrals. stonemasonry like that of Giotto's bell tower. and lattice-topped pies.

Jane Howard

Thank-you notes are, in the purest sense, an expression of the person who writes them. They are, in actuality, a small piece of the sender. You can jot down a quick note saying thanks for the birthday gift an old friend of the family sent from Florida, but take that even a step further, and the opportunity exists to really brighten someone's day, or perhaps even improve someone's life.

By nature, members of the human family like to be appreciated for what they do. Rare are the individuals who are so fortified by their own beliefs that they need no acknowledgement or appreciation. When we tell someone that we have noticed the kind, efficient, or honest things they do, we can effectively reinforce that behavior while making them feel great about who they are and how they act.

Although it is becoming increasingly easy to forget in this age of drive-throughs, automatic tellers, and voice mail; human beings are social animals. We need to make connections with each other. Writing a thank-you note makes a connection and brings a relationship full-circle. It may seem like a simple thing, and it is, but it is often the simple things that make life worthwhile.

When to Send a Thank-You Note

Event	*Essential or can I decide for myself?*
Wedding gifts	Obligatory, within three months—even if verbal thanks have been given.
Mailed gifts	Yes, this is mandatory within two to three days from when gifts are received. Even if the gift received was a thank-you, the sender wants to know it arrived safely. Give them peace of mind.
Birthdays, Christmas, and other gift-giving occasions	Easy one. A note should be mailed within two to three days from when the gift is received.
Wedding or baby shower	As in other gift situations, a note is in good taste and shows appreciation to the giver.
A dinner party	A note is always a good idea, and will probably guarantee you an invitation again sometime.
Staying with friends	A note is important. Close friends or family may be happy with a phone call of thanks, but they really deserve better. Send a card!
Gifts or help during an illness	When you are feeling up to it, a note is a must.
Receipt of notes or flowers of condolences	Always send one. Always. Someone was concerned for you, express your appreciation.
Business gifts or entertainment	Never a must, but you do want to make that sale, right? You want to bet on the winner? A note can only help you foster a good relationship with clients, fellow employees, or your boss.

3

How to Write
Thank-You Notes

A thank-you note is an act of grace. It completes a circle. If I take the trouble to tell you, on paper, what a difference you have made to me, then it makes your gift, or kindness, an act of mutuality. It is something between us, something we share. It connects us, and makes us both feel not only better, but possibly saner.

Jane Howard

Now you are getting down to the actual writing; that nitty-gritty process of putting pen to paper. For most people, this is the point at which anxiety attacks or minds go blank. In the 'how to' of writing thank-you notes, there are really only a few elements to consider.

❖ Are there rules of etiquette for the gifts for which you are saying thanks? If it is a wedding gift, you need to be aware of the protocols. Other events for writing thank-you notes have some fairly flexible rules, and you should write accordingly.

❖ A thank-you note should be handwritten except in the case of e-mail. The length of the note can vary. Wedding thank-you's are generally rather short, as can be other notes in which you are saying thank-you for a gift. But if you are writing a note to a dear friend whom you just visited, why limit yourself? Your relationship with the person to whom you are writing will often dictate length. A novel is probably not a good idea, but then neither is a one-line letter of five words.

❖ The five basic elements for writing a thank-you note should include:

1. Address the individual(s), using a salutation or greeting. Refer to Salutation on page 14 for additional information.

2. Say thank-you.

3. Identify the gift (be certain to get this one right. It does not look good to thank Mr. and Mrs. Smith for the lingerie when they sent you a toaster.)

4. Express how you feel about the gift and what it will be used for.

5. Add a personal note or message.

6. Sign your thank-you note. Refer to Signature Line on page 15 for additional information.

Within this framework, there is a great deal of latitude. When preparing to write a note, sit for a moment and consider your relationship with the person to whom you are writing. Is it intimate and personal? Is it someone you know as an acquaintance? Are you writing to a complete stranger? This should dictate the tone of the note you are writing.

Think about exactly how you feel regarding the gift or favor for which you are thanking someone. This can be very difficult to do when you are writing five hundred wedding thank-you's in two days, but otherwise, it should determine what you say and how you say it.

There is no need to be afraid of genuine feelings. This is what makes your thank you an individual and valuable expression of yourself.

At this point, you should have a more complete understanding of how you can use your own personal feelings to express gratitude and brighten someone's day.

Examples of thank-you notes have been written for a variety of circumstances and are included in each chapter. Use these examples as inspiration and adapt them so that they apply to your individual situations.

Example of a thank-you note using the five basic elements.

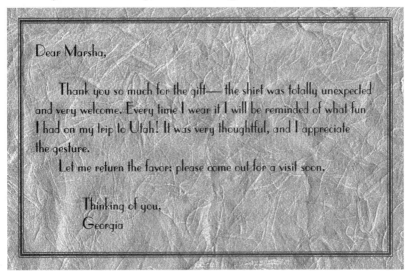

Dear Marsha,

Thank you so much for the gift— the shirt was totally unexpected and very welcome. Every time I wear it I will be reminded of what fun I had on my trip to Utah! It was very thoughtful, and I appreciate the gesture.

Let me return the favor: please come out for a visit soon.

Thinking of you,
Georgia

Points to Keep in Mind

1. Why are you writing? What is the purpose of the note?

2. To whom are you writing? One person, a couple, a family?

3. What is your relationship? Business, friend, or family?

4. How about personality? Does the person have a keen sense of humor?

5. What kind of tone do you want to convey? Formal or informal? Personal? You should be sincere, specific, and positive.

6. Is your writing clear and concise? Check for spelling and grammatical mistakes. Always reread your note.

Salutation

The salutation or greeting that you use when writing a thank-you note is based on the formality of the occasion and your personal relationship to the recipient.

For informal situations, such as close friends and family, a first name or nickname is appropriate.

For more formal situations and to acquaintances, the following conventions should be followed:

❖ Women may be addressed by Miss, Mrs., Ms., Madam, or by a professional title. Use whatever the woman herself prefers. If you are not certain, use Ms.

Men are greeted by Mr. unless they have a professional title. A good reference, if you are not certain how they would prefer to be addressed, is to see how they signed any enclosed cards or notes.

❖ Traditionally, married couples are addressed by the husband's first and last name. However, this is changing since many women prefer to be addressed by their first name, or keep their maiden names after marriage. It is appropriate to address the couple using both of their names:

Dear Mr. O'Donnell and Ms. James,

This is also the appropriate way to address unmarried couples.

❖ When writing to couples where one or both of them have professional titles, you should always address the title first in a formal situation if the person prefers to be addressed that way:

Dear Dr. and Mr. Lavos,
Dear Drs. Lavos,
Dear Dr. Ricardo Lavos and Judge Claire Lavos,

Signature Line

The signature line or complimentary close of a note also depends upon the formality of the occasion and your relationship with the person to whom you are writing.

❖ For formal situations, such as writing to government officials or members of the clergy:
> *Respectfully yours,*
> *Respectfully,*

❖ In the case of less formal relationships or when writing to institutions, government agencies, businesses, or acquaintances:
> *Very truly yours,*
> *Yours truly,*
> *Very cordially yours,*
> *Very sincerely yours,*

❖ Use informal signatures when writing to friends, family, and for informal occasions:
> *Sincerely,*
> *Sincerely yours,*
> *Best wishes,*
> *Cordially,*
> *Regards,*
> *Love,*
> *Kindest regards,*
> *Your friend,*

For formal situations, you should sign your full name, such as John Doe, rather than John. For informal situations, sign your name as you prefer it.

Note: When a woman writes a thank-you note before her wedding, she should sign her maiden name, even if she is planning to change her name after the wedding.

4

Wedding Thank-You Notes

Thank-you letters often sound like exercises in etiquette, but in the hands of a gifted writer, a thank-you note can sound like a good short story.

Lois Wyse

It is a little-known and seldom-discussed fact that a newlywed from Columbus, Ohio, once stuck his entire hand into a functioning toaster to avoid having to write "Thank-you for the toaster" for the thirty-third time.

If properly managed, the entire experience of writing wedding thank-you notes can be far less painful than it was for the man who is now left-handed.

Be aware of protocol; this may be the only category where the omission of a thank-you note could cause a serious strain on, or even ruin, a friendship. Wedding thank-you's are mandatory, and you will not be easily forgiven if you choose to ignore this little ritual.

The secret to writing successful wedding thank-you's is to strike a balance between a form letter and personal letter. You need to follow some kind of form in order to keep your sanity when faced with a seemingly endless number of thank-you notes, but each note needs to sound personal and sincere.

Be aware that every person that gave you a gift or helped you with wedding plans did so with thoughtfulness, good intentions, and you in mind. Your thank-you's should reflect their thoughtfulness.

❖ Consider the gift, a toaster is not particularly personal, but what are the characteristics of a toaster? Can they be related to the giver of the gift? A toaster browns things, it makes things pop up, some of them are extra wide for bagels, some of them are ovens . . . the list goes on.

❖ Consider the giver, some of them you know well and have a close and probably informal relationship with. Some of them—especially in the case of weddings—you may have met for the first time at the reception, and the thank-you note will be more formal. Do any of the characteristics of the gift match those of the giver?

This note is pretty informal, maybe even silly, but it is personal and will make Jonathon smile when he reads it—and it will make him remember you and your relationship. The point is, Jonathon knows that the note was written especially for him. He feels that the person writing it is grateful and gracious, and that is how you want him to feel. Remember, you can get away with being a little silly, especially in an attempt to make a friend feel special. But writing a cold, insensitive form note will only inspire the receiver to read it quickly and put it in the trash.

There are situations where relating the gift to the giver is not a great idea. How would Mr. and

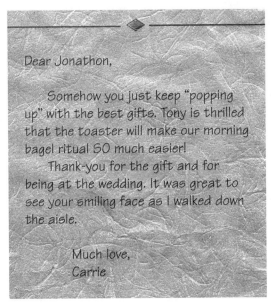

Dear Jonathon,

Somehow you just keep "popping up" with the best gifts. Tony is thrilled that the toaster will make our morning bagel ritual SO much easier!

Thank-you for the gift and for being at the wedding. It was great to see your smiling face as I walked down the aisle.

Much love,
Carrie

Dear Mr. and Mrs. Rogers,

Thank-you so much for the beautiful crystal vase, it is by far the nicest piece of art in our new living room! I promise to keep it filled with flowers throughout each and every year!

It was wonderful to see you at the wedding. Congratulations on your 50th anniversary! We both consider the two of you an example of married life worthy of imitating.

Best wishes,
Albert & Vanessa Francisco

Mrs. Rogers feel if you referred to them as "cold and hard like fine crystal?" Besides, the relationship here is obviously less intimate, and should be handled as such. A good idea is to mention something specific about the gift and how you will use it, and say something personal about the giver and/or your relationship. As always, take the time to think about the person(s) to whom you are writing.

There should not be any confusion in how to write a wedding thank-you note because we are telling you to "create a form" and "write something personal." You can easily come up with the perfect thank-you by evaluating what the gift is, from whom it came, and what your relationship is to the person. After a while, you will be writing thank-you notes faster than Grisham can write his novels!

There are a few additional protocols associated with wedding gifts and thank-you's. Standard etiquette is that those invited to a wedding have up to a year after the blessed event to offer a gift. However, you do not have that long to respond with a note of appreciation. All thank-you notes should be sent within three months following the receipt of the wedding gift; and truthfully, would you not want to have it completed as soon as possible?

Traditionally, wedding gifts are sent to the bride and she writes the thank-you notes signing them herself, but mentioning the groom's name in the body of the note.

The times are changing, however, and grooms are sharing the writing of thank-you notes with the bride, especially for gifts sent by his friends and relatives. A note from him would be far more personal than a note from the bride who may be almost a stranger. The thank-you may be signed by the writer or from both the bride and groom.

Take the time together to consider each gift and giver. It is the perfect opportunity to spend some time with your new spouse. Get your favorite beverage and a snack, let your creative juices start flowing, and have fun!

Dear Paul,

Who would have thought you had such good "taste" in kitchen items?! We love the mugs and assorted coffees. We have already brewed up a pot of the Chocolate Hazelnut—couldn't resist!

As soon as we return from Thailand, you must come over and help us enjoy "all" that a good cup of coffee has to offer!

Much love,
Cherie and Sid

Wedding Note #1

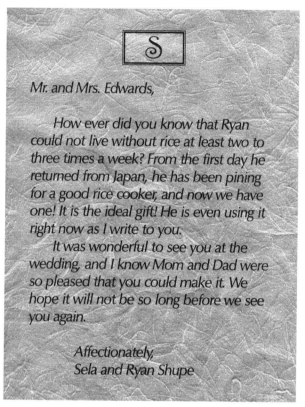

Mr. and Mrs. Edwards,

How ever did you know that Ryan could not live without rice at least two to three times a week? From the first day he returned from Japan, he has been pining for a good rice cooker, and now we have one! It is the ideal gift! He is even using it right now as I write to you.

It was wonderful to see you at the wedding, and I know Mom and Dad were so pleased that you could make it. We hope it will not be so long before we see you again.

Affectionately,
Sela and Ryan Shupe

Wedding Note #2

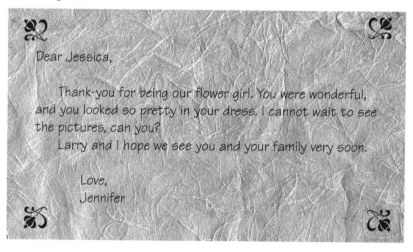

Dear Jessica,

Thank-you for being our flower girl. You were wonderful, and you looked so pretty in your dress. I cannot wait to see the pictures, can you?

Larry and I hope we see you and your family very soon.

Love,
Jennifer

Wedding Note #3

Dear Elaine and Jack,

What a perfect gift for a couple with so many pictures. The picture album is not only beautiful, but so very unique—it looks just like us!

When things finally do settle down, we will fill it with all of the pictures of our most memorable days. Until then, it is perfect on the coffee table as is!

Many thanks,
Mark and Deborah

Wedding Note #4

Dear Mom and Dad,

Words cannot describe what we feel for both of you. Now that the wedding is over and things have calmed down somewhat, we wanted you to know how grateful we are for everything. You have done more for us than we could ever repay. Your love, support, and prayers have always been felt, and we sincerely appreciate it.

Now, in the years to come, as we prepare to have our own children, we hope and pray we can be half the parents and friends to them that you have been to us.

Thank-you for being the best mom and dad any child could ever hope to have!

All our love,
Bob and Katie

Wedding Note #5

Dear Father McConnell,

Words cannot describe how we feel about the wedding ceremony that you performed on our behalf. Obviously, weddings are deeply personal events, and we so appreciated your flexibility and willingness to work with our ideas.

We were especially touched by the personal anecdotes that you collected from members of our families and told during the lighter moments of the ceremony.

Thank you for giving us the gift of a beautiful beginning to our life together.

Sincerely,
Greg and Lisa Brady

Wedding Note #6

Dear Mr. & Mrs. Rothschild,

The Waterford Crystal candlesticks you sent are exquisite and a perfect match to our stemware. I look forward to setting our table with your gift as a most beautiful centerpiece.

Thank-you for your thoughtfulness.

Sincerely yours,
Karen Austin

Wedding Note #7

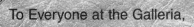

To Everyone at the Galleria,

Thank you all for a perfect gift! Cooking is something Maria and I love to do together, and the set of cookbooks will keep us busy and our menus constantly changing for a long time!

In fact, we will try a new recipe or two very soon and bring them to the Galleria to share.

Thanks again,
Maria and Alec

Wedding Note #8

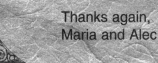

Dear Annie,

Of all the gifts we received on our wedding day, yours was perhaps the most thoughtful. This being the second marriage for both of us makes it more special and more difficult at the same time.

We look forward to reading *The Second Time Around*. A quick perusal has shown the book to cover just the things that have caused us both some concern thus far.

Thank you so much for caring enough to recognize a gift that we could really use.

All of our love,
Blake and Crystal

Wedding Note #9

Dear Mrs. Logan,

Had I known how much work planning my own wedding would be, I might have thought twice about doing it all on my myself.

You may have had the same thoughts after I asked you to make the wedding cake. However, I cannot be sorry for asking you, because the cake was truly spectacular and just what I wanted.

Ever since that Thanksgiving when Melissa brought me from college to your home, I have always thought of it as my "home away from home." You were always there for me during those years in college when my own family was so far away.

Being a starving college student, your home-made Thanksgiving and Easter dinners were something to look forward to, but it was your cakes and pies that I will never be able to forget!

Thank you for agreeing to make the cake and putting so much time and effort into it. I was so very pleased when I saw it; I could not have imagined anything more beautiful and delicious!

Once again, you were there for me when I needed you. Thank you for everything you have done over the years, but especially for this latest and most appreciated "labor of love."

Forever,
(Mrs.) Sandra "Rainer"

Wedding Note #10

Dear Ben,

Wow! I never knew you could look so great in a tuxedo. I believe some of the young female guests were paying more attention to you than to either the bride or to me, the debonair groom.

Even so, there is no denying that you performed your duties as usher with sophistication and flair. If there were any moments of hesitation—"Do I seat her on the left or right? Will this older gentleman be able to make it down the aisle to his seat? Is my boutonniere on straight?"—it did not show.

You were grace under pressure, and I was both honored and proud to have you in my wedding party! Thank you for doing a great job and helping to make everything go so smoothly.

Maybe I will still be around to usher people at your wedding—if you ever get married!

Fondly,
Kirk

Wherever you are, it is your own friends who make your world.

William James

5
Gift Thank-You Notes

Gratitude takes three forms: a feeling in the heart, and expression in words, and a giving in return.
Proverbs

The receipt of gifts in a variety of situations and for a wide array of events should be responded to within two to three days. Always consider your relationship with the sender when sending a thank-you note.

1. Mention the gift, what you will do with it, and how it makes you feel.

2. Add a personal touch by writing down how you feel about the sender or talk about what you have been doing and what life has brought you.

3. Remember a past shared experience, allude to a familiar joke, or a mutual acquaintance.

The rules for the varying types of thank-you notes are easily interchangeable and quite often identical. The secret is to put a little bit of your personality on the paper; that is what people will be most happy to see in the notes they receive.

Birthday Gift Note #1

Erica,

You are absolutely the craziest person I have ever known! I do not know why I am thanking anyone for sending a male stripper to me at work, but let us just say we must both have the same great sense of humor. It was an absolutely fantastic gag, even if it was on me!

All I can say is you better be more than a little wary when your birthday rolls around—for the rest of your life! You will never know when I am going to strike, and you may have to live with that! Thank you, but I will "get even."

Your tormented friend,
Bruce

Birthday Gift Note #2

Dear Jose,

As I said at the time, your thoughtfulness in choosing my birthday present was very much appreciated. I have wanted something to put all of my paintings in, forever. I could never figure out the best way to display and protect them at the same time. The plastic "envelopes" of the carrying case will do both.

You are a good friend, and I am so lucky to have you around. Thank you very much.

Love,
Tabitha

Birthday Gift Note #3

> Dear Grandma,
>
> Thank-you for the check you sent for my birthday. I have had my eye on a new pair of running shoes, and with the money you sent, now I will be able to get them.
>
> I really loved the card you sent. You always manage to find the perfect sentiment for every occasion. I am looking forward to seeing you at Mom and Dad's on Thanksgiving.
>
> Love,
> Andrew

Graduation Gift Note

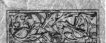

Dear Mr. and Dr. Sanchez,

Thank you very much for the graduation check. It was so very generous of you. As you know, I will be leaving for NYU in the fall, so the money will certainly come in handy. I have already deposited it into my "textbook fund."

Thank you, also, for your advice about medical school, Dr. Sanchez. I have not yet decided, but I promise you that I will seriously think about it.

I hope to see you this summer sometime before I leave!

Sincerely,
Jennifer Chen

Baby Gift Note #1

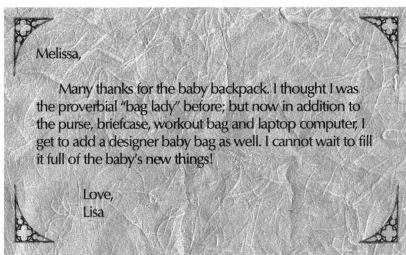

Melissa,

Many thanks for the baby backpack. I thought I was the proverbial "bag lady" before; but now in addition to the purse, briefcase, workout bag and laptop computer, I get to add a designer baby bag as well. I cannot wait to fill it full of the baby's new things!

Love,
Lisa

Baby Gift Note #2

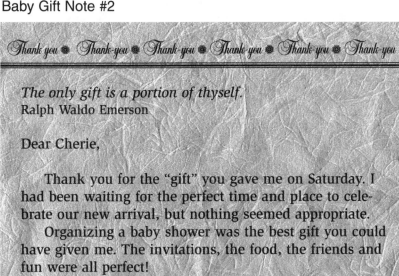

The only gift is a portion of thyself.
Ralph Waldo Emerson

Dear Cherie,

Thank you for the "gift" you gave me on Saturday. I had been waiting for the perfect time and place to celebrate our new arrival, but nothing seemed appropriate.

Organizing a baby shower was the best gift you could have given me. The invitations, the food, the friends and fun were all perfect!

It makes me so very happy to have a friend willing to give so much of her time the way that you did.

All my love,
Lee Anne

Baby Gift Note #3

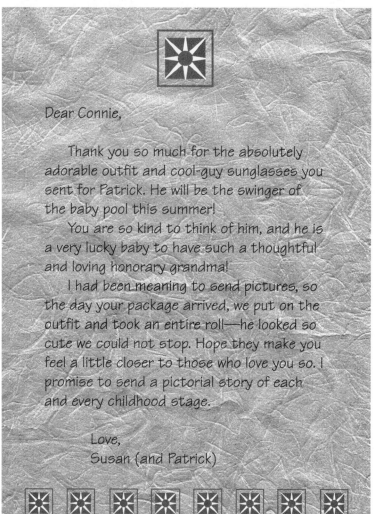

Dear Connie,

Thank you so much for the absolutely adorable outfit and cool-guy sunglasses you sent for Patrick. He will be the swinger of the baby pool this summer!

You are so kind to think of him, and he is a very lucky baby to have such a thoughtful and loving honorary grandma!

I had been meaning to send pictures, so the day your package arrived, we put on the outfit and took an entire roll—he looked so cute we could not stop. Hope they make you feel a little closer to those who love you so. I promise to send a pictorial story of each and every childhood stage.

Love,
Susan (and Patrick)

Only by thinking of me with your heart, could you have given such a special gift.

Anonymous

Anniversary Gift Note

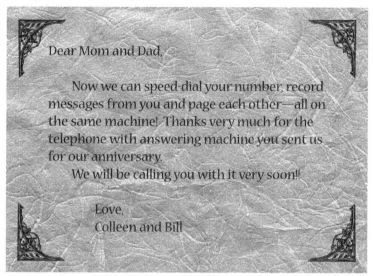

Dear Mom and Dad,

Now we can speed-dial your number, record messages from you and page each other—all on the same machine! Thanks very much for the telephone with answering machine you sent us for our anniversary.
We will be calling you with it very soon!!

Love,
Colleen and Bill

Christmas Gift Note #1

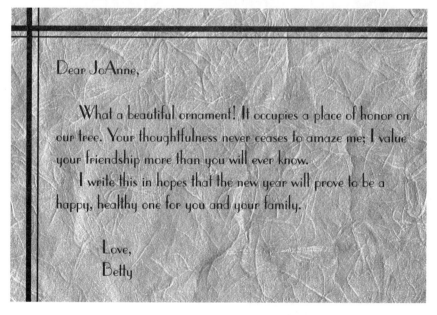

Dear JoAnne,

What a beautiful ornament! It occupies a place of honor on our tree. Your thoughtfulness never ceases to amaze me; I value your friendship more than you will ever know.
I write this in hopes that the new year will prove to be a happy, healthy one for you and your family.

Love,
Betty

Christmas Gift Note #2

Dear Mother,

Just when I was feeling old and cynical, and wondering if Santa could possibly exist, I was surprised by your present. I opened the box, pulled back the tissue paper, and promptly burst into tears. Charles thought I had uncovered a box of cut and nicely packaged onions.

I just could not believe my tear-washed eyes. Where did you ever find her? I thought Daisy had been lost forever. How did you know that holding this precious doll would bring back a flood of tender memories. To be reunited with my childhood friend, keeper of my secrets, is just what I needed. I love her even more this Christmas than I did on that Christmas so many years ago when you gave her to me for the first time.

Thank you, Mother. Who needs Santa when I have you?

Love,
Clara

God could not be everywhere and therefore he made mothers.

Jewish Proverb

General Gift Note #1

Dear Aunt Judy,

My thanks go on and on—just like the jigsaw puzzle! It is perfect for the long winter nights ahead. You are so good at puzzles. I wish I had you up here to help me with this one (hint, hint).

I cannot wait to get started, so sign me...

Puzzled in Montana!
Annie

General Gift Note #2

Reece,

Uh, I guess I should start by admitting that I feel a little strange saying these things to you. My wife says I am getting in touch with my feminine side—whatever that means? Anyway, I want to say thank you for remembering the gold pocket watch I liked so much when we were antique shopping in the Midwest. It means even more coming from you. You have always been such a good friend.

Gratefully,
Aaron

General Gift Note #3

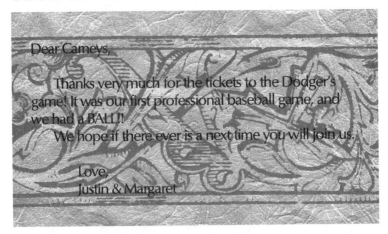

Dear Cameys,

Thanks very much for the tickets to the Dodger's game! It was our first professional baseball game, and we had a BALL!!

We hope if there ever is a next time you will join us.

Love,
Justin & Margaret

General Gift Note #4

Bob,

I will concede to you that when I opened your gift, I was actually a little angry—by the gift of running shoes—that perhaps you thought I have a small weight problem and could probably benefit from a little more exercise. Actually, all of my feelings were mixed because you were absolutely right.

Well, in the two months since you gave me the shoes, and while I have been quietly fuming at you, I have also been running regularly. Now, 15 pounds later, people compliment me, my wife finds me more attractive, and some old clothes actually fit. I feel great!

True friends are the ones who find a kind and diplomatic way to tell you the truth. It only took me 500 miles to realize that.

Thank you for being a true friend,
Sean

6

Hospitality Thank-You Notes

Kind words are the music of the world. They have a power which seems to be beyond natural causes as though they were some angel's song which had lost its way and come to earth.

Frederick William Faber

Think about the last time someone welcomed you into their home, fed you, allowed you to sleep late, entertained you, and stimulated you with conversation. Usually in these types of situations, it is exactly these qualities in hosts that make guests so comfortable the guest is lulled into failing to send a note of thanks after the visit has ended.

Perish the thought, and get into the habit of writing notes. Hospitality could be very basically defined as being shown a good time; a warm welcome by friends, family, or proprietors; and the sharing of what others have with you.

The most obvious examples of these types of hospitality involve friends and family—your best friends from college offer you their cabin on the lake for a weekend; your aunt and uncle put you up in New York for a week and give you a tour of the city; your mother and father invite you to stay for a week to recuperate from a particularly rough year.

Additionally, the owners of small hotels and bed and breakfast inns have made it part of their charm and livelihood to create an environment in which guests feel as if they are staying with friends or family. A note to these people would also be appreciated and well received.

Informal and lively, notes offering thanks for hospitality can be creative, expressive, and a lot of fun. Recount the way you were made to feel by the hospitality shown you. What memories do you have of the time you spent? At what moment did you feel particularly relaxed and at peace with yourself and the world? What small act did the person to whom you are writing perform to make you feel more comfortable and at ease?

Thank-you notes for hospitality, whether it be for a nice evening and dinner or for a week's stay at someone's house, should be sent immediately—the next day for a dinner or within a couple of days following any lengthy stay. Also, it is customary to include a small gift with the note for stays with friends or family longer than overnight; something that is personal and thoughtful shows that you were paying attention to more than

Dear Rachel,

I am quite certain that for the rest of my life, the smell of lavender will remind me of staying in your guest room, so please put this little lavender plant someplace where it will remind you of how truly thoughtful and sweet I think you are.

We had such a wonderful time during the ten days with you; the restaurants were fabulous; the late night chats between us over too much red wine allowed me to open my heart and let a friend in; and the drive up the coast was perhaps the most beautiful trip I have ever taken.

Next time it is our turn. We want to see you both very soon, so put aside some time when you can stay awhile. Chicago is perfect in the spring! We would love to show you around! Thank-you again for everything, but most of all for being my friend.

Love you both,
Rob and Sheila

just how soft the bed was or how good the food.

Some great ways to say thank you for hospitality include sending postcards from the next leg of an extended trip or picking up a coffee table book from an interesting place visited during the trip.

Of course, with friends and family, a reference to your being the host at some time in the future is probably wise and rather natural. When writing to a business of some sort, you might mention that you will recommend the establishment highly to people you know. The greatest compliment you can pay a business is high praise.

If you feel someone has been hospitable to you, send them a gracious thank-you. It truly is one form of payment for the hospitality that you have received.

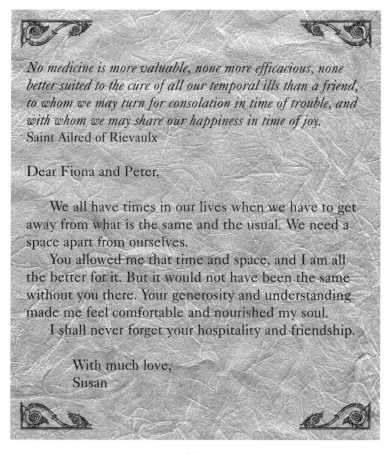

No medicine is more valuable, none more efficacious, none better suited to the cure of all our temporal ills than a friend, to whom we may turn for consolation in time of trouble, and with whom we may share our happiness in time of joy.
Saint Ailred of Rievaulx

Dear Fiona and Peter,

We all have times in our lives when we have to get away from what is the same and the usual. We need a space apart from ourselves.

You allowed me that time and space, and I am all the better for it. But it would not have been the same without you there. Your generosity and understanding made me feel comfortable and nourished my soul.

I shall never forget your hospitality and friendship.

With much love,
Susan

Hospitality Note #1

Dear Mr. and Mrs. Feldman,

It was very generous of you to share your home with us. We were afraid that because of unexpected expenses, we would not be able to take a family vacation this summer, and we hated disappointing Sara and Justin. Your offer of the beach house at Newport came at the perfect time, and we all thank you sincerely for making our summer vacation possible.

Both Sara and Justin—and their new summer friends—had as much fun playing under the avocado trees in the backyard as they did playing and running on the beach. They were most unhappy to learn that we will not live there year round!

I hope that we will have the chance to thank you in person and that we can offer to you what you have so generously given to us.

Sincerely,
Dave, Susan, Sara & Justin

Hospitality Note #2

Dear Melissa and Steve,

How do I thank you...let me count the ways! I thank you for the great talks over coffee; for the wonderful and unselfish hospitality; for the Mother's Day gift; for chauffeuring me around so I could see so many new sights; for cooking one gourmet meal after another; and for a million other things, including just being two of the greatest children a mother could ever hope for.

I really had a perfect time with you both and look forward to being with you again in September. I hope this time you will let me spoil you just a little.

I will call this weekend.

Love,
Mom

Hospitality Note #3

Your warm hospitality is rivaled only by the grace of its ministration.
Anonymous

Dear Deborah,

You and Ken are such wonderful hosts. Once again, Judy and I can only tell you that there is no other house where we have such a good time and hate to leave so much. We especially enjoyed the party Saturday evening and meeting all of your friends.

Thank you very, very much for including us, and Judy joins me in sending much love,

Gary

Hospitality Note #4

A house may draw visitors, but it is the possessor alone that can detain them.
Charles Caleb Colton

Dear John,

Thanks for delaying me! Your new place at the lake is beautiful, and there is so much to do. I had forgotten how much I enjoy water-skiing until we were actually out on the water.

But it is true, the best part of a visit to your house is the getting to see you again and the catching up on what has been happening in your life. It is too bad we are not able to get together more often.

Next year it is your turn to come to my place so I can repay you and your hospitality!

Talk to you soon,
Ashley

Hospitality Note #5

Charlie,

Just a very late note to say thank you for joining us for lunch while Sara and I were in New York. You always add that which is missed when you are not there.

Sara loved meeting all of you—it is always nice to put a face to the name she so often hears!

Love,
Jo

Hospitality Note #6

Dear Randy and Amy,

Dinner last night was splendid, as, of course, was your company. I never cease to be amazed at the wide variety of topics that come up in conversation when I am around you two. Last Saturday night was no exception.

You continue to be such an important part of my life. I am blessed to have you both for friends.

Please let me reciprocate soon.

Thank you, and love,
Leslie

Hospitality Note #7

Greetings Kellie and Dave!

Hands down, the sound of chirping birds beats honking horns any day! Thanks for giving us the chance to "get back to nature." Your cabin is perfect for those wanting to "rough it" in style!

I noticed you have every John Irving book but this one. *The Hotel New Hampshire* is one of my favorites, although it does not compare in comfort to your beautiful hideaway.

Enjoy, and thank you again!
Darren

7
Condolence Thank-You Notes

Uncle Virgil was one of the most adored men I have ever known. Not only did adults like me gravitate to his smiling countenance and generous spirit, but the children in the family, including my son, considered him the pied piper. We will miss him—

Anonymous

As many axioms try to teach us, friends are not made during good times. True friendships are forged of difficulty and strife. Those people who must go through unfortunate and tragic loss in life soon learn of true friends and are eternally grateful for all that they do and who they are.

If you have suffered the loss of a friend or family member, you will write thank-you notes when you are ready to do so. Nothing should really spur you to act any sooner than your emotions allow. Friends will understand.

When it comes time to sit down and thank people for showing support, empathy, and caring, let them know how much you appreciate their thoughts and why. Not everyone is capable of knowing how it feels to lose someone close or how difficult your trials are, and still others who do not know how it feels, but are aware that you are in pain and want to try and lessen that, should know that you are grateful.

The thank-you note you write in association with expressed condolences will probably be a bit longer than most. There are a few details you will want to include when thanking people for their concern.

1. Be certain to specifically thank people for what they said. Let them know that you read, heard, and took to heart the words they wrote, especially if they too have suffered the loss of someone close—those are the friends who will be there and suffer beside you.

2. Spell out how you feel about your loss or trials, and how you are coping with it. The people who wrote notes to you did so out of concern, and they will want to know about your progress.

3. Mention the individual whom you are mourning in a way that is funny or warm. As you progress in your life, you will always want to remember people you have lost in positive and meaningful ways. Including a memory or anecdote of that person serves two purposes in a thank-you note; it tells the person receiving your note that you are well on your way to healing and recovery, and it gives that person your permission to also remember and perhaps speak of your lost loved one in similar, unobstructed ways.

4. In conclusion, it is probably wise to express something positive. If you do not yet feel ready to end your message on a high note, then perhaps the time has not arrived for writing, but this is strictly a personal judgment call.

Each situation will be different, but if you have lost someone close to you, it is possible and probably healthy to use the writing of thank-you notes as part of the healing process. Emotions that may have been decidedly negative, or at least pent up and tormented, will want to escape and express themselves, as emotions are wont to do, but remember to express the positive. Use writing and the expression that comes with it as a cathartic experience.

Condolence Note #1

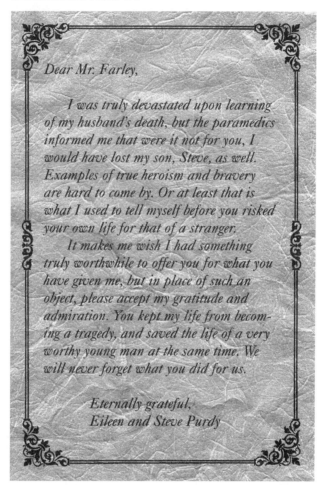

Dear Mr. Farley,

I was truly devastated upon learning of my husband's death, but the paramedics informed me that were it not for you, I would have lost my son, Steve, as well. Examples of true heroism and bravery are hard to come by. Or at least that is what I used to tell myself before you risked your own life for that of a stranger.

It makes me wish I had something truly worthwhile to offer you for what you have given me, but in place of such an object, please accept my gratitude and admiration. You kept my life from becoming a tragedy, and saved the life of a very worthy young man at the same time. We will never forget what you did for us.

Eternally grateful,
Eileen and Steve Purdy

Instruct me how to thank thee.

Elizabeth Barrett Browning

Condolence Note #2

Brian,

These days I often think about the the last few months and how much my life has changed. I do not think I could have done it alone.

Watching my father's condition worsen was the most difficult thing I have had to do. Just being able to talk about it and be heard meant everything to me, and you always came around to check in on Mom and me. I am overwhelmed by your concern for us and the compassion you demonstrated.

I would like you to know that we would like to help you in any way we can, should you ever need it. You are truly a kind and generous friend, and you have touched our lives.

Thank you,
Eric and Donna Baker

Condolence Note #3

Dear Mr. and Mrs. Patton,

I remember a time when Rick and I had a long discussion about death. I told him how afraid of death I am, but he only talked about living life with energy and focus, and he said living that way made him not fear death. I think he believed that every minute of his life.

I know that the circumstances of Rick's death are tragic, but I will always remember how he lived life. Your condolences are very much appreciated because I know you too will remember how he lived. Thank you for that.

Fondly,
Megan Christinson

Condolence Note #4

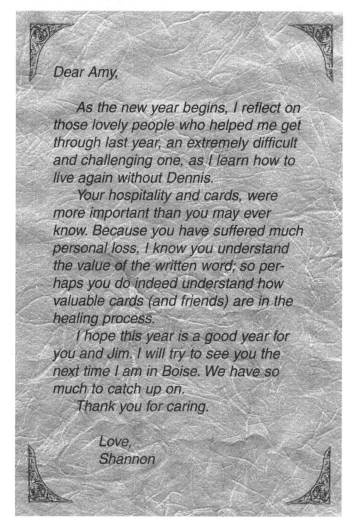

Dear Amy,

    As the new year begins, I reflect on those lovely people who helped me get through last year, an extremely difficult and challenging one, as I learn how to live again without Dennis.

    Your hospitality and cards, were more important than you may ever know. Because you have suffered much personal loss, I know you understand the value of the written word; so perhaps you do indeed understand how valuable cards (and friends) are in the healing process.

    I hope this year is a good year for you and Jim. I will try to see you the next time I am in Boise. We have so much to catch up on.

    Thank you for caring.

          Love,
          Shannon

One kind word can warm three winter months.
Japanese Saying

Condolence Note #5

Dear Mr. Parsons,

I think it is very important that you know I do not hold you responsible for the death of our yellow lab, Ranger. I know that accidents do happen, and I was very touched that you picked him up and took him to the veterinarian immediately after the incident.

My father told me how badly you feel about the accident, and that you still feel responsible. Ranger was the kind of dog that loved to run and play. We had trouble keeping him in the yard, and he was almost hit several times before. That it happened while you were driving is simply bad luck.

Please do not feel badly any longer. I appreciate you trying so hard to help him.

Sincerely,
Lucy Edwards

Real unselfishness consists in sharing the interests of others.

George Santayana

Condolence Note #6

Kind words are the music of the world. They have the power which seems to be beyond natural causes, as though they were some angel's song which had lost its way and come to earth.
Frederick William Faber

Dear Martha,

Your kind words did indeed have the power of an angel's song. There were many times during the worst days of my illness that your words were in fact all that I could hear.

Your prayers and encouragement were often what gave me just enough resolve to make one more effort. Even when I had decided that nothing in life was worth the pain I was experiencing, you reminded me of why I had to try harder.

I can never thank you enough for getting me through those days and standing by me today. You really are my angel on earth.

All of my love,
Sadie

What I do not owe you!
Jane Austen

Condolence Note #7

Dear Don and Tracy,

It is an unfortunate truth that "the rough times" are part of everyone's life. This ancient lesson is now so painfully clear.

We have also learned what real friendship is. You offered to loan us money, help Don get a job, take the children for an evening, and cook us dinner. While we may have declined your help at the moment, it was purely out of pride and embarrassment. How grateful we are, now, to know how much you care and what wonderful people you both are.

Now that we are back on our feet financially, it is easier to see the future with a clear head and better focus. Know that we are always here for you, and that we love you for the help you offered.

Your devoted friends,
The Thomases

Condolence Note #8

Thank-you for feeling "with" me rather than "for" me.
Anonymous

Richard,

I cannot thank you enough for the calls you made immediately after I lost my job and continue to make even now. I really thought it was the end of the world when they told me I was being "let go." In a way it was the end of my world, but you were the one who convinced me that it was not necessarily a bad thing.

I see things in a completely different way, I have more opportunities than ever before, and I feel more positive and in control. Those changes are due mostly to your weekly, sometimes daily, phone calls. Thanks also go to your wife for putting up with my sometimes desperate calls and your—I am afraid— large phone bills!

Thanks for your help in putting the pieces back together.

Your friend,
Todd

Thank you. You helped me not only find my place in life, but my way home.
Unknown

8

Kindness and Service
Thank-You Notes

I knew the little Mexican woman who cleaned our offices spoke little English. so I took it upon myself to recall just a portion of my college Spanish and write a brief note one evening. leaving it tacked to my desk. I really cannot say exactly what inspired me to write the note. "Gracias por la limpiar." it said. How

If I pose the basic question to you, "what is the purpose of writing a thank-you note?" you will probably respond with, "to say thanks." You would, of course, be absolutely correct. A thank-you note is intended to show appreciation, usually for a gift or service done on your behalf.

Consider for a moment the thank-you note as a medium for showing kindness and for improving someone else's life, even if for the most brief of moments. A great many people perform their daily tasks in relative obscurity and without so much as a hint of appreciation, and over time this often takes a toll on the human psyche. You may be able to improve a life or change the way one person treats another. At the very least, you may make someone's day just a little better.

Bear with us for just one moment as we illustrate the psychological perspective which is the foundation for the "thank-you notes can change lives" theory. We already touched on the idea—above and in the introduction of the book—that human beings are, by nature, in need of affirmation and appreciation. If you are a doubter of this belief, simply perform a very basic experiment. Present a thank-you card to someone you see regularly but are not friends with, such as a bus driver, a waiter, the cable guy, or the woman who clips your dog. Watch their reactions, and then decide again whether you think people like to be noticed for what they do. Thank-you notes are the perfect way for you, as an individual, to affect change.

Consider, for example, a young man who was working his way through college by waiting tables in a downtown restaurant. On any given day, men and women very much concerned with their own lives and jobs would fill the restaurant shortly after noon, give abrupt orders and vacate the establishment almost as quickly as they had arrived. But on one particular day, the young man returned to clear the table of a customer who had been eating alone to find a business card accompanying the tip.

embarrassingly basic. I hurriedly left before she arrived. afraid that I was slaughtering her language. Two nights later. as I was leaving the office around seven. the woman approached me. took my hand and with her charming spanish accent said. "You welcome." To this day. I cannot recall having heard such beautifully spoken English.

David Macfarlane

> *Thank you for your great service! Your attitude will get you anything you desire and are willing to work for.*
> *Sheldon*

With a simple gesture, Sheldon J. Weisfeld of Houston, Texas, had restored the morale and redeemed the character of at least one individual. Chances are good, Sheldon does that sort of thing all the time and very much enjoys it.

Is there a style or protocol for writing thank-you notes for service or kindnesses? No, not really. As explained previously, talk about that for which you are grateful. It is so easy in this situation to nail down exactly what to say because you would not be writing the note at all if you did not have something specific to say thank you for. It is probably a good idea not to get too personal with people you do not know well, but other than that, let your conscience be your guide.

One fun idea is to keep a selection of postcards to drop in the mail when you want to say thank you to someone. You can jot down something simple.

but words expressed on paper are fantastic. Even a short note means so much.

The people to which you write need not be strangers or acquaintances. Certainly you have friends who would appreciate a note just to cheer them up. In fact, the opportunities to thank friends and family for their acts of kindness are probably much more numerous. Though we tend to take those close to us for granted, we receive help from others constantly, and they would surely appreciate a note of thanks. Nothing elaborate or lengthy is necessary. See the note below as an example of something simple, expressive, and to the point.

Dad,

Michael and I thank you for bringing the tomatoes from your garden. Summer would not be the same without them! We love you.

Jo

How simple was that? The beauty of this type of thank-you note is that they are usually unexpected, and always appreciated. Good thoughts are great,

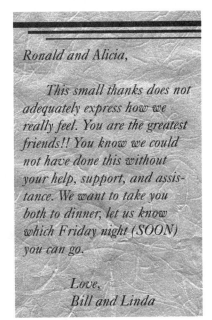

Ronald and Alicia,

This small thanks does not adequately express how we really feel. You are the greatest friends!! You know we could not have done this without your help, support, and assistance. We want to take you both to dinner, let us know which Friday night (SOON) you can go.

Love,
Bill and Linda

While a brief note may make the day or week of the person to whom you send a note, thinking in terms of others and how they may feel could alter your entire life. A simple change of habit can reap huge rewards in the long run. Besides, what do you have to lose? And what could you potentially gain?

Kindness and Service Note #1

Dear Frank,

Thank you for sending the beautiful flowers. They arrived yesterday afternoon, when it was so wintry and dark and cloudy. When the delivery man came, it was just as if the sun had come into the living room. Each time I pass by them, they remind me of you. I wish you were here so that we could enjoy them together, but rest assured that I will enjoy them enough for the both of us.

An extra bonus is the beautiful vase that holds the flowers. In the spring, I will fill it with gladiolus and sweet williams, and be reminded of your caring all over again. Please know how much you have brightened my days. Thank you again for remembering me.

Love,
Julie

Kindness and Service Note #2

Dearest Irina,

"It is not so much our friends' help that helps us, as the confident knowledge that they will help."
Epicurus

I always know I can count on you.
Thank you, thank you, thank you!

Love,
Beth

Kindness and Service Note #3

Dear Patti,

I must sit down and put pen to paper to tell you how much your call yesterday afternoon meant to me. For some reason that I am unsure of, it had been one of those down days. To unexpectedly express my doubts and concerns to a friend, and know that she would sift through them and let the chaff blow away, was such a comfort and reassurance to me. Somehow exposing our fears to the light makes them seem that much less frightening.

Now, we must go to lunch and enjoy some happy times. But remember, I will always be grateful that you took the time to listen to me. Talking is sharing, but listening really is caring. Thank you again for caring so much.

With a grateful heart,
Cecilia

Kindness and Service Note #4

Dear Martha,

Certain people touch our lives in such a special way, that anytime they are in our thoughts, it seems a special day! I feel just this way about you!!! You will never know the impact you have had on my life. I wish there were words to express such feelings. I only hope you can feel of my love and appreciation for you. Thanks, for just being you.

Much love,
Erica

Kindness and Service Note #5

*Without friends no one would choose to live,
though he had all other goods.*
Aristotle

Dear Jeff,

The older I get, the more I realize how important my friends are to me. If only it did not take advanced age to gain wisdom!

Thank you for always being around when I need you, for never expecting anything in return, and for caring unconditionally. I consider myself blessed indeed to be a friend of yours.

May you have the best always,
Tim

Kindness and Service Note #6

"We are crazy. People have said it. We know it. Yet we go on. But being crazy together is just fine!"

Ray Bradbury

Dear Kathy,

It is kind of funny in a way. While the rest of the world is driving me insane, you alone remind me that it is perfectly all right to be just a little bit crazy. You help me laugh at this maddened world. And you remind me that being perfectly normal is not as important as I believed it to be. You teach me to cope by letting go, and you put my list of priorities in perspective. Thank you for convincing me to burn my "To Do List" and to hide my day planner in the drawer. You know, on days like today, it really does help. I am happier than I was before. I have remembered how to play.

On my fifth life and loving it more and more . . .

Your friend,
Rebecca

I wanted someone to laugh with me—how do I say thank-you?

Anonymous

Kindness and Service Note #7

Dear Hannah,

I thought about you all last Tuesday. I hope you are doing well and that you have had a good week. I really do miss having you near.

Thank you for all you have meant in my life. There have been many times I have cried on your shoulder—both in reality and in my mind.

The days fly by and I do not do as I should, but know that you are very special to me.

I hope your family is well and happy.

Your friend,
Diane

Kindness and Service Note #8

Dear Ms. Fatima Salamda,

I do not know when I have enjoyed a flight as much as my recent travel on Thai Airlines Flight #570, L.A. to Bangkok. Usually, I dread those long, international flights, but you made me so comfortable, I was honestly quite surprised at how quickly the travel and time passed.

Finding the newspapers and magazines I like, bringing me a cup of tea "after hours", giving advice on where to go and what to see in Bangkok...

Thank you for doing your job so well and even more for all those things that are above and beyond the call of duty.

Sincerely,
Beverly Hansen

Kindness and Service Note #9

To The Woman Who Brings My Newspaper,

Every morning for the past two months, I have opened my door and found my newspaper tucked inside the screen. At first I thought the newspaper had assigned a new delivery person, or changed their policies on deliveries to older people. But then, one morning, I saw you pick up my paper on your morning jog and deliver it directly to my front porch.

This small and unexpected act of kindness is one that means a great deal to someone such as me. Bringing the paper to my porch may seem like such a simple thing, but to someone who has suffered a broken hip, it is anything but easy. Many days I labored for thirty minutes getting the paper before you came along. Some days I just never made it at all.

You probably wanted to remain anonymous, but I just could not go another day without thanking you. The newspaper keeps me in touch with the outside world, and is so important to me. Perhaps one day you can stop by and stay for tea. I would love to get to know you better.

Gratefully,
Melba Jorgensen

Kindness and Service Note #10

Dear Mr. Jefferson,

The first time I sent my son off to catch the bus to school on his own, I was not sure I was going to survive the beginning or the remainder of the day.

Knowing that Simon is on your bus, in your hands, makes me feel so much better! Thank you for taking such good care of all of our children, each and every day. My husband, my boss, and the other parents thank you, too!

Sincerely,
Mrs. Joan Pettit

Kindness and Service Note #11

Gimme a "T"
Gimme an "H"
Gimme an "A"
Gimme an "N"
Gimme a "K"
Gimme an "S"

Coach Sloan,

Even though we did not win the State Championship, it was an exciting year! You are the greatest coach ever! Thanks for all that you did for the cheerleading squad, especially the end-of-season dinner. We know that next year will be even better.

Love,
Highland High Cheerleaders

Kindness and Service Note #12

Dear Mrs. VanDyke,

I was asked today who my greatest influences were as a beginning writer, and the first name that came to mind was yours. It may seem funny, I did not think of Shakespeare, or Faulkner, or even Austin; I thought of you. I learned more during that one short year of senior English than I have learned in my entire life. You taught me that English could be more than grammar, spelling, and diagramming sentences. For you, English was, and I imagine, still is a rich tapestry of stories that stretches from man's very beginning out as far as our potential will take us.

You taught me to read deeply, to absorb, and enjoy the written words; but most importantly to write from my heart.

Through you I learned to appreciate even the trivia of literature. I will never forget the yellow wall paper in *Crime and Punishment* or Emma Bovary's pet greyhound. But most of all, I will never forget you, or all you did for each of your students. You saw our potential and helped us grow. I do not know how to thank you. Words alone will not do. I owe so much to you.

Sincerely,
Amanda Erickson

Kindness and Service Note #13

Dear Coach Malone,

On behalf of all of the parents whose children played on your T-ball team, I want to thank you for a memorable season. You are one of the few coaches I have met who truly believes in developing a love for the game of baseball and places the "winning" of the game in proper perspective. You have helped each child explore his potential while building his self esteem.

As a mother of boys, I have seen more than one approach to coaching, but yours is the one I most appreciate. Your strong coaching skill is not really a skill at all; it is a part of your character. You value the children, it is really that simple. My husband and I are truly grateful you had room in your schedule and heart to become a part of our son's life.

With gratitude,
Marjorie Henry

Kindness and Service Note #14

Dear Aunt Marlene,

It was so nice to receive your Christmas card and best wishes for the New Year. Thank you for thinking of us.

We moved to West Kaysville, and we were so pleased your card found us. We are all fine—Michael and I are alone, with all the children gone now.

We so hope all is well with you. You are still such an inspiration to all of us. We hope the new year is a wonderful year for you—Thank you again.

Much love,
Lorna and Michael

Kindness and Service Note #15

Dear Grandmother,

Your phone call struck a chord in me that is still vibrating as I write now. "Remember me? I am your grandma," you asked me over the miles. Remember you? Why of course I do! But, after we talked and said our "good-byes," I realized I should do more than just remember. I want to thank you for my memories and let you know just how much you mean to me.

How could I forget you, Grandmother, it was you who gave me my first taste of homemade ice cream. You watched smiling as I ate too much, and then you kissed me sweetly, not minding my sticky little face.

Every summer, you filled my room with fresh cut roses taken from your prized bushes. You calmed me as I fretted at what I thought was a waste of their tender blossoms. It was you who taught me even though cut roses die, the joy they bring lasts forever in our memory.

Each night you pulled me up in your lap and rocked me gently before the fire. You sang to me songs your grandmother sang to you. In gentle whispers, you shared stories of your youth. Now, I have children of my own and though you cannot be here, I share with them all I learned from you. My ice cream will never be as sweet, nor my roses as fragrant, but the songs I sing and the stories I tell will bring back lessons you helped me learn. Nothing you did was ever wasted, Grandmother, for the joy you brought me I try to give to others.

I realize I often take for granted the people who mean the most to me. I have waited far too long to tell you how much I love you. Thank you for being such a beautiful part of my life.

Love always,
Bridgette

Kindness and Service Note #16

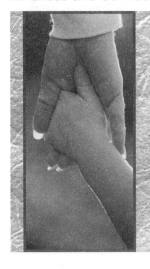

Dear Mom,

Sometimes one picture says Thank You far better than a thousand words.

Love,
Marla

Kindness and Service Note #17

My dear little Amber,

I miss your sweet smiles, your soft snores, and even your smelly diapers. I have been trying for hours to concentrate on contracts and proposals, when I would so much rather be home playing with your little toes.

When I left you with Mrs. James for the first time today, I knew she would take care of you just the way I would. Our sweet neighbor has raised five children of her own, and now she is directing all of her love to you.

You have added a whole new level of happiness to my life. I never imagined I could love someone so small, so much.

I am fully aware you will not be able to read for some time. But when you can read and understand, you will read this little note and know how much I truly love you. I want you to know going back to work was not a decision I made lightly. I want you to understand how much I would rather be with you. Thank you for giving me a reason, the best reason, to rush home. I cannot wait to see you!

Love,
Mom

Kindness and Service Note #18

Dear Mother,

I know you were here just a few short hours ago, but I have to write to you now to say the things I could not say then. Samantha is sleeping softly now. When I listen closely, I can hear her gentle breathing in the tiny bed beside me. She is more beautiful than I ever could have imagined, but you knew she would be.

I was so frightened of this whole miraculous process, but you and Jeff got me through it all. Mom, I just do not know how to thank you. Gazing at this sweet, soft, brand-new baby, I guess I am realizing for the first time what you have felt for all of your children. If I can only be half as loving, half as hard-working, and half as patient as you have been, this small child will truly be blessed.

I am so happy, but at the same time, I am still very anxious. I never really comprehended all that you have done, not until now. Can I hope to do it all, too? I am so grateful I have you to turn to. Perhaps one day you and I will look back on my fears and smile. Until then, I will muddle through hoping to be just like you.

Love,
Karen

We take for granted the very things that most deserve our gratitude.

Cynthia Ozick

Kindness and Service Note #19

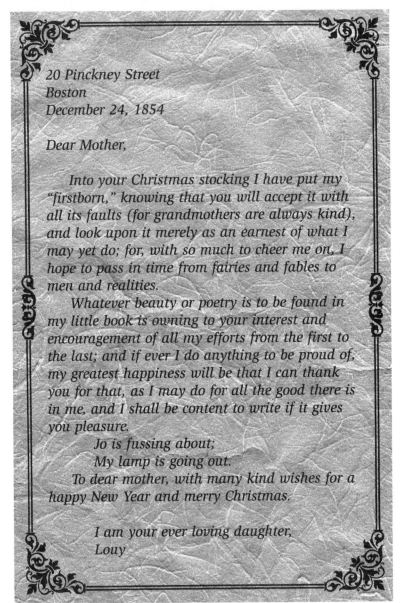

20 Pinckney Street
Boston
December 24, 1854

Dear Mother,

Into your Christmas stocking I have put my
"firstborn," knowing that you will accept it with
all its faults (for grandmothers are always kind),
and look upon it merely as an earnest of what I
may yet do; for, with so much to cheer me on, I
hope to pass in time from fairies and fables to
men and realities.
Whatever beauty or poetry is to be found in
my little book is owning to your interest and
encouragement of all my efforts from the first to
the last; and if ever I do anything to be proud of,
my greatest happiness will be that I can thank
you for that, as I may do for all the good there is
in me, and I shall be content to write if it gives
you pleasure.
Jo is fussing about;
My lamp is going out.
To dear mother, with many kind wishes for a
happy New Year and merry Christmas.

I am your ever loving daughter,
Louy

Louisa May Alcott sent this thank-you note to her mother
along with a copy of her first book, *Flower Fables*. Alcott
used her mother as a model for the well-loved Marmee in
one of her most famous books, *Little Women*.

9

Children and Thank-You Notes

At last it was time for the party to end. Lowly remembered to say to Dolly and her mother. 'Thank you for a very nice time.' He is a very polite [worm]. isn't he?

And what does Lowly say when someone gives him something?

THANK YOU!!'

From Richard Scarry's "Please and Thank You Book."

We all want to give our children the tools to succeed in life—to make many friends and handle social situations with gratitude and grace. It is with that thought in mind that children should be encouraged—or perhaps required, depending on your view of encouragement—to begin writing thank-you notes as soon as they can read and write.

By teaching your children to write thank-you notes as early as possible, you will be doing them a lifelong favor. "Thank you" is one of the first concepts learned by children, and often they can express surprisingly mature thoughts and feelings. Writing them down may require a little help, but it should be fun, and it will be beneficial at not only a young age, but throughout their life.

Consider, for a moment, the child who attends the birthday party of your son or daughter, and later sends a brief note thanking you for having them, or the child to whom your son or daughter gives a birthday gift and then mails your child a note of appreciation. The note may be somewhat illegible—perhaps even unintelligible—but for you as a parent, how impressed are you with this young person who took the time to say thank you? Even the cynic must acknowledge that a

67

child who is coerced into writing a thank-you note is learning important habits and the value of expressing appreciation.

Through this simple act, a child begins to see the value of their actions to someone other than themselves. Who would not be proud to have a more selfless and feeling child? There are lessons to be learned in simply writing thank-you notes.

The following are very simple thank-you notes that a child could use in order to become familiar with the style. As time passes, practice will take the place of the steps, and then eventually, habit will pick up where practice left off. The purpose of the form is to offer some sort of structure; it is not intended to eliminate a child's personal expression. As always, the note should include something personal between the child and the recipient. Let the children go, and see what they come up with. In all likelihood, the results will usually be both hysterical and educational.

Just think of the improved relationships you will have as a result of your child's exemplary behavior. People will think you are a great mother and father.

① say thank-you

② say how you feel about the gift

③ add something personal, funny, or nice

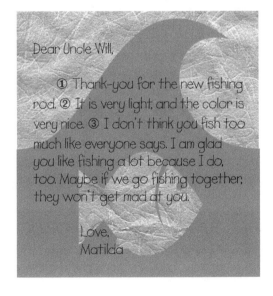

Dear Uncle Will,

① Thank-you for the new fishing rod. ② It is very light, and the color is very nice. ③ I don't think you fish too much like everyone says. I am glad you like fishing a lot because I do, too. Maybe if we go fishing together, they won't get mad at you.

Love,
Matilda

Children Note #1

Dear Grandma,

Thanks for letting me stay at your house while my mom and dad were in Hawaii.

I had a really great time, except when you made me eat green beans. But that's okay, because I know they are good for me. The best part was when we went to the zoo. I think you must be very smart, because you knew everything about all the animals!

I hope my mom and dad go on another trip soon so I can stay with you again.

Love,
Tim

Children Note #2

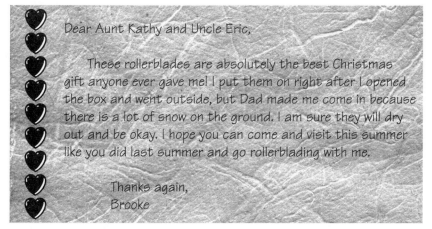

Dear Aunt Kathy and Uncle Eric,

These rollerblades are absolutely the best Christmas gift anyone ever gave me! I put them on right after I opened the box and went outside, but Dad made me come in because there is a lot of snow on the ground. I am sure they will dry out and be okay. I hope you can come and visit this summer like you did last summer and go rollerblading with me.

Thanks again,
Brooke

Children Note #3

Dear Aunt Linda,

I am writing this note to say Thank You for letting me spend some of my brightest and most unforgettable times with you. Since the day I was born, you have come to mom's house, swept me up in your arms, and carried me away to a magical time and place that can be visited only when I am with you.

The summer weekends and the winter vacations I spent with you and Uncle Dave are the highlights of my childhood memories. In your home I have always felt completely free to explore, discover, and play. You encouraged me to get my hands dirty and make a mess. "After all," I can still hear you say, "true creative genius is never neat, organized, or contained."

For all of these things, and for the books and ideas with which you filled my mind, I will always love you.

Thank you for everything, but most of all, for belonging to me.

Love,
Lisa

Children Note #4

Hi Uncle Andy,

The new skateboard is killer—just what I wanted. I have been riding it all day, and it is smooooth!

My friend found a rad place to ride, so I'm going to try some tricks. I will let you know how I do.

Thanks a lot!
Marty

P.S. My mom says that if I break my neck, she's sending you the bill!!

Children Note #5

Dear Uncle Steve,

Thank you for letting me carry the ring for Aunt Margie at your wedding. I didn't like wearing that tuxedo very much, but everything else was fun. And I am glad you did not get hurt when you fell when the preacher asked you that question. Didn't you know the answer? I feel that way too when my teacher asks a question and I don't know the answer. I want to visit you soon.

Love,
Ricky

Children Note #6

Dear Grandpa Charlie,

You make me so happy! When you come to visit, I can never wait to jump up on your lap. I love the way your tickly whiskers always brush against my face when you kiss my cheek.

I especially like your stories. I know you were so scared to go away to war when you were a young man. But, you did it anyhow cause you knew it was what you were supposed to do. I hope when I am big I will be just as brave as you.

I like that story you tell about my daddy and that big mean, red bull. I can hardly believe he was ever little like me, but I see him in my mind when I listen to you. Thanks for being such a great grandpa!

Visit soon, love,
Teddy

Children Note #7

Dear Jordan,

Your party was fun. I liked it. Thanks!

From,
Mike

Children Note #8

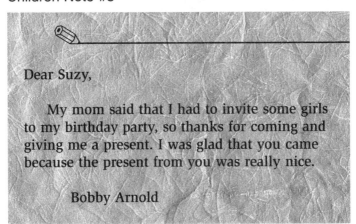

Dear Suzy,

My mom said that I had to invite some girls to my birthday party, so thanks for coming and giving me a present. I was glad that you came because the present from you was really nice.

Bobby Arnold

Teach us to give and not to count the cost.
Ignatius Loyola

Children Note #9

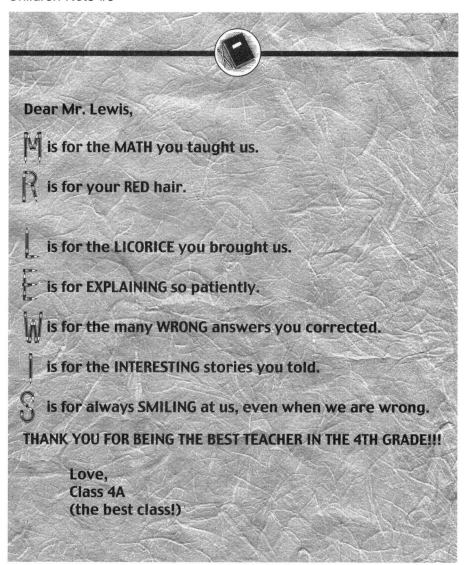

Dear Mr. Lewis,

M is for the MATH you taught us.

R is for your RED hair.

L is for the LICORICE you brought us.

E is for EXPLAINING so patiently.

W is for the many WRONG answers you corrected.

I is for the INTERESTING stories you told.

S is for always SMILING at us, even when we are wrong.

THANK YOU FOR BEING THE BEST TEACHER IN THE 4TH GRADE!!!

Love,
Class 4A
(the best class!)

Children Note #10

Dear Mr. Edwards,

Thank you very much for teaching me this year. I liked your class a lot, especially when you read us stories after lunch. My favorite story is the one about the fuzzy bear. I think he looks like you.

I am a little scared about going to 4th grade. I hope Mrs. Hill is as nice as you. Can I come back to your class and see you some time?

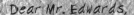

Love,
Amy Jenson

Children Note #11

Dear Coach Bryant,

I know that you get frustrated because I always strike out, but I think you are a good coach, so Mom said I should write you a note to say thank you.

You never yell at me, and you always just say nice things and tell me that next time I will get a hit. Maybe I won't, but you always say that, which is nice.

Thank you,
Mary Louise Allanson

10
Business Thank-You Notes

That best portion of
a good man's life,
His little, nameless,
unremembered acts
Of kindness and of
love.
William Wordsworth

This is where the kindly art of writing thank-you notes wanders into the area of the more practical. Generally, thank-you notes are thought of as messages between friends and family.

The cynical view notes of thanks from businesses as nothing more than a blatant attempt to get us to come back and spend more money. But there really is nothing wrong with being friendly to try and win repeat business.

The first thank-you note from a business was sent by a crotchety old guy named Gerald Spencer who opened a hardware store in Tacoma in 1923. Peeved that his neighbor Jim had come into the store and had only purchased a bag of nails, Gerald fired off a simple note expressing his disgust and sarcastic wit.

> *Thanks for spending money in the store. Next time spend a lot more.*
>
> *Gerald Spencer.*

The irony was lost on Jim, and he thought the note was wonderful; so he told his family and friends about it, and business at the store exploded.

From those humble beginnings, however, grew current marketing and public relations practices. The idea is to add a personal touch to what can, at times, be such an impersonal process. For the conscientious and committed salesperson, writing notes of thanks is an excellent way to convey a genuine quality and sense of commitment to both your product and your client. If you maintain that relationship with a client by mailing a note and business card, the chances improve they will remember you the next time they are in need of whatever it is you provide.

You have probably received this particular brand of thank-you if you have made a major purchase, or sent one if you sell sizable items.

Consider writing notes to the superiors of people in business with which you are particularly pleased. Not only will it strengthen their positions, it could also eventually lead to advancement and a raise for these people. Unsolicited thank-you's and positive feedback may mean a lot when it comes time for policy and decision making, and promotion decisions.

You can jot down a quick note to a contractor whose work you are especially pleased with; a boss who governs with an even and well-tempered hand; the coach who teaches your kids the true value of sportsmanship.

It goes without saying that showing appreciation is simply good business, whether you are the consumer or the supplier. And

---

D & D Furniture

Dear Mrs. Evans,

I will bet you are cooking more happily now than ever before! I do most of the cooking in our house, and know that the brand and model range you purchased is a fantastic tool in the kitchen. I just wanted to say thank you again for choosing Dawson Furniture for your major appliance purchase. If you should have any problem at all with the item you purchased, or when you need to make additional purchases, please come back and see me and I am certain I can make you happy. Enjoy your new range! Happy cooking!

Sincerely,
Brad Davis
D & D Furniture

while it may seem that the world in general, and the business world in particular, are becoming more and more impersonal, logic holds that the foundation for business is still society; society is made up of people and people must communicate. Hence, the more personal contact individuals have, the better the potential for success in any relationship.

As always, when writing a note, mention the item or service for which you are thankful and how it makes you feel. In the case of professional relationships, also say something about how the relationship will be influenced in the future. Will your company provide service? Will you be back to shop again? Will you recommend the person or business to friends and family? Professionally, thank-you notes will make the difference between you and everyone else when it comes time for the consumer to make a business decision.

Business Note #1

Dear Mr. Reinhold,

On July 3, my husband and I came to Hubbert Auto to shop for a new car. Having visited and been frustrated by salesmen at many other car dealerships, we cannot tell you what a breath of fresh air your new salesman, David Hayes, was to work with.

David applied the least amount of pressure I have ever experienced in an auto salesman. He presented the benefits of the car (which we purchased), and then allowed us private time to make a decision. When it came time to write the purchase, David patiently negotiated on our behalf for two hours before an agreement was reached. He is truly an asset to your company, and we will recommend you to family and friends. We will return to you to purchase another car because of him.

Sincerely,
Beth and Ken Rickard

Business Note #2

Dear Amy,

Buying your first car is a most memorable and lasting moment, and I wanted to say Thank You for allowing me to be a part of the experience. I still remember my first car—a little yellow Volkswagen with black interior and an eight-track tape player. That car took me and my friends through college and many great experiences together, and I am certain your Jeep will do the same for you.

I hope that your purchasing experience with our dealership was a good one, and want you to know that we will be there for you in the future as well. Enclosed, please find one of my business cards. Do not hesitate to call me should any problems arise with your Jeep. We pride ourselves on our record of service after the sale, and our award-winning service department is at your disposal should you need assistance.

When it comes time to move on to another vehicle, or if a friend is looking for a car, please tell them about the experience you have had with us. Good luck, and I look forward to seeing you again in the future.

Sincerely,
Bob Larsen
Sales Manager

Phone (801) 555-1212 • 245 E. 500 South • Park City, Utah

Business Note #3

Best Host Inn

San Jose, California

Dear Mr. Simmons,

I want to thank you for selecting the BestHost Inn for the members of your wedding party. I appreciate it very much and look forward to having them stay as our guests.

I have enclosed the contract for your review. Please read it over, sign one copy and return it to my attention. I have enclosed one copy for your records. If you have need to make any changes, do not hesitate to call me at 1-800-555-2211.

Again, thank you, and be assured we will make your guests' visit a comfortable one.

Sincerely,
Kathy Howard
General Manager

He who thanks but with the lips
Thanks but in part;
The full thanksgiving
Comes from the heart.

J. A. Shedd

Business Note #4

Theresa Mitchell's
Scenes of Nature Gallery

Dear Mrs. Linda Wolf,

Thank you for visiting Theresa Mitchell's Scenes of Nature Gallery in Park City. We sincerely appreciate your support of Theresa's limited edition photography.

By now you should be enjoying "Amboselli Crossing Elephants" in your own home. If there is anything more we can do for you, please do not hesitate to contact us. We look forward to having you return to our gallery in the future.

Laura Alleman
Gallery Manager

Business Note #5

Hillary,

Thank you so much for the information on the Santa Barbara Museum of Natural History. I was, frankly, touched that you had remembered my interest based on our brief meeting.

I am going to save the bulletins and use them to plan an "escape" with some friends this summer.

Regards,
Janna McBride

Business Note #6

Dear Graffiti Removal Team,

It is not often that I feel motivated to write to a public organization, and when I do, it is usually to complain rather than praise. However, on behalf of those who, like me, never write complimentary notes, I would like to thank you for the great job your organization is doing.

I live in an area that, while safe, sees its fair share of graffiti. There has not yet been an instance when your organization was called that you did not respond in a timely manner. I am certain that you are kept quite busy, so it is even more impressive that within a week the graffiti disappears.

Thank you for a job well done! There are many (silent) citizens who appreciate it!

Sincerely,
Diane Cordova

Business Note #7

Holly,

What can I say except what I have said so many times before?! It is always so good to see you—you bring a smile to my day, and a little prayer of thank you that I have the greatest job because it is filled with friends like you. You are talented, wise beyond your years, and truly one of the nicest people I know. Thank you for letting me call you friend.

Marcie

Business Note #8

Dear Adria,

A short, late note for a couple of reasons—first to congratulate you on a great sales conference and catalogue. Your job is not an easy one and you need to know how much all you do is appreciated. Second, an apology for misintroducing you to Sara. Of everyone there, I know your name the best because you are my favorite—by far one of the nicest!

Please forgive me and understand it was because my mind was so cluttered with so many details!

Have a great summer and I will see you in the fall.

Love,
Joyce

P.S. If you cannot read this, call me, and I will see if I can translate! My writing is obviously not in much better shape than my memory!

Business Note #9

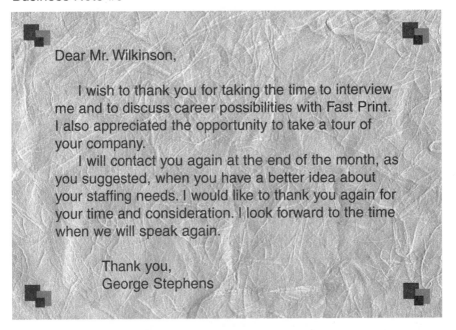

Dear Mr. Wilkinson,

I wish to thank you for taking the time to interview me and to discuss career possibilities with Fast Print. I also appreciated the opportunity to take a tour of your company.

I will contact you again at the end of the month, as you suggested, when you have a better idea about your staffing needs. I would like to thank you again for your time and consideration. I look forward to the time when we will speak again.

Thank you,
George Stephens

Business Note #10

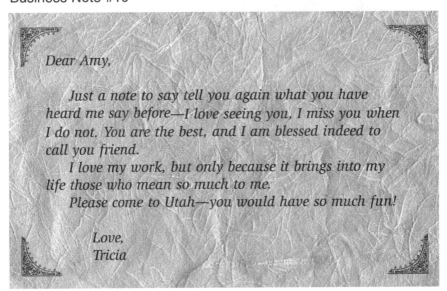

Dear Amy,

Just a note to say tell you again what you have heard me say before—I love seeing you, I miss you when I do not. You are the best, and I am blessed indeed to call you friend.

I love my work, but only because it brings into my life those who mean so much to me.

Please come to Utah—you would have so much fun!

Love,
Tricia

Business Note #11

"Behind every great man is a surprised woman!"
Maryon Pearson

Dear Mr. Simmons,

I must say, if I ever believed the above statement, you changed that opinion in me forever. The work you did remodeling our home was absolutely fantastic.

I was, admittedly, very nervous about each and every contractor who bid on this project. My home is a sanctuary for me, and I am very particular about what happens to it. Of course, you already know this, because at every turn I was there to critique and evaluate your work.

Although I was quite satisfied with your work upon completion of the project, I am now closer to elated. Every time I enter a room I notice a new detail that you added. Your craftsmanship is unlike any I have ever seen. You know your work, you took the time to know me, and you combined those pieces of knowledge into something marvelous. This has become the home of my dreams, and I am quite certain we will never leave it!

Sincerely,
Frances Farnsworth

Business Note #12

Dear Mr. Schmidt,

Though it feels somewhat strange writing a letter to someone I have never met, I both needed and wanted to write a letter thanking you for loaning my family and me the money to purchase a new home. I know this is an act you must perform daily, and perhaps you are seldom aware of how you touch individual lives.

This place that I call home is absolutely everything to me, and this particular house is one I have watched and waited on for years. You have fulfilled a dream for me, and I look forward to filling my new home with the love and laughter of family and friends.

May your holiday season be filled with happiness and love, and may the New Year bring you, in return, as much as you give to others, which is so much. My prayer is that God may bless you.

Thank you,
Christine Hart

Business Note #13

Dear Shawn and Rita,

I am both pleased and content to see such a lovely family buy my home. This house is so much more than four walls and a roof to me. I love every square inch of it.

You will have years and years to fill this place with memorable experiences of your own, as your children and their friends explore, learn and grow. I am pleased that you will continue the legacy of children and grandchildren swinging from the trees and rolling in the grass.

I was reluctant to put my home on the market, but when you visited and asked me personally about the memories the home holds for me, I knew it was the right thing to do.

Thank you for helping me through what was a difficult decision—I know you will be happy here.

Gratefully yours,
Sally Wayment

Business Note #14

Dear Frank,

I just wanted to say thank you for all the little extras you do for me throughout the year. Duffy loves the bones you save for him, and you always seem to know which cuts of meat I will like best.

There are not many butchers these days who give such personal service. Please be certain of how much you are appreciated.

Until next time,
Mimi Rogers

Business Note #15

To Amy, the paper girl:

Thank you very much for doing a terrific job delivering our newspaper. We have rarely had any problems, and when we have, you were there immediately with a solution. We really do appreciate your hard work and being so responsible.

Sincerely,
Mr. and Mrs. Cook

P.S. I hope you like chocolate chip cookies. If not, let me know, and I will make your favorite next time!

Business Note #16

Dear Allen,

Thank you for mowing my lawn each week. You do a really nice job, especially when you clean up all the clippings from the sidewalk.

I used to love taking care of my own yard, but I am not able to push a lawn mower anymore. I am happy about our business arrangement because you can earn a little money and I can still have a beautiful yard!

Sincerely,
Mrs. Alfred James

11

Internet and E-mail Thank-You Notes

No matter how far apart we are, you always manage to remember me. Thank-you for making me a part of your lie wherever you are.

Anonymous

We will start with a few basic observations about communicating via the World Wide Web:

❖ Etiquette on the Internet is informal. Sometimes very much so.

❖ Salutation and closing or signature lines are not necessary, but can be used to create more personal communication.

❖ Short one- or two-sentence paragraphs can be used, separated by an extra line space, to make your message easier to read on the screen.

❖ DO NOT USE FULL CAPS. On the Internet, this is the equivalent of shouting, and is really one of the few forms of behavior (other than direct e-mail marketing) that draws fire from other users. Full caps are also harder to read.

Although we usually think of the written word as being more formal than the spoken, e-mail is perhaps the one instance when this does not necessarily hold true. E-mail and the internet in general tend to be informal and often irreverent means of communication.

It is not as easy to embellish your e-mail messages since you will not be able to use stationery, stickers, stamps, colored pens and pencils, or fancy signatures.

The nature of the Internet is something like the Wild West, though not as much as it once was. Using it can be exciting, creative, adventurous, and a great deal of fun, especially if you take advantage of all that the technology has to offer. For those of you who are not familiar with computers or the Web, it is not difficult to learn. Try the following format and you will probably see that it is not all that intimidating.

Subject: Thanks for the great evening!
Date: Sun, 28 Jun 01:37:13 -0600

To: carol@quickmail.com
From: midori@quickmail.com

If you do not give me the recipe for your pasta salad, you will never see the card table and chairs I borrowed from you ever again!

This may seem like quite a drastic step, but your recipe is that good.

I had a great time at your BBQ last night. The food was fantastic, the conversation stimulating, and the weather perfect. The first two I know you had a hand in, but how did you manage the third?

Thanks so much for a fun evening. It was great to see the old gang again...not that any of us are really THAT old! I will give you a call this week, but I did not want to wait to tell you how much I enjoyed myself. Hello to Jason and the children.

There are a few things to be noted in a thank-you sent via e-mail, such as the sender, recipient, date, time, and subject (if provided) that are immediately apparent, even before looking at the message. Some individuals feel that the salutary and signature lines—or "To" and "From"—are, therefore, unnecessary. Others feel it makes the message more personal, and it can be a hard letter-writing habit to break. The decision is up to you. There is very little formal or written e-mail etiquette to date.

Although there are few rules and protocol concerning e-mail, it is wise to observe some type of structure when it comes to writing e-mail thank-you notes. Very little is written about this, but common sense offers a little insight into what is appropriate.

❖ Use e-mail to send only informal messages or to respond in kind. The e-mail message on page 89 is a good example. The recipient will appreciate the note because it is a kind gesture and probably not expected. On the other hand, if you receive a lovely gift or handwritten letter through the mail, you should not send off a quick e-mail to say thank-you.

Respond with your thank-you in the manner by which you received the gift or card.

❖ Do not assume that you can use e-mail to send a thank-you for every occasion. Weddings and condolences are two situations that will demand more formal and respectful protocol.

Consider to whom you are writing and if that person is comfortable using a computer and receiving e-mail. Your grandmother may have a computer and know how to use it, but would she rather get an e-mail message from you or a kind, handwritten note on paper?

Various websites allow you to put personalized information into a greeting card format that you choose. In this way, you may personalize your "communication," which in turn may impress your friends and family. The person to whom you send this cybercard will receive a message in their e-mail telling them they have a card, and instructing them how to get it. It is as simple as that.

The internet opens doors to new choices and a considerable number of options.

E-mail Note #1

Subject: Thank-you!
Date: Sun, 28 Jun 01:37:13 -0600
To: dmmac@vision.postech.edu,beth@yipee.com,
e_smith@penn.edu,bottle@moonshine.com
From: cotson_d@ugu.ut.edu

I know I have said it before, but I want to say it at least once
again . . . thank you for a job well done! It was because all of you
worked so hard that this year's presentation was a success.

I wanted to let you know right away that the board has accepted
our proposal, and the project should get underway very soon,
barring any further bureaucratic steps that need to be taken.

I will get a copy of the most recent report to you shortly, and
accept, just one more time, thank you!

Debbie

E-mail Note #2

Subject: Hello!
Date: Sun, 28 Jun 01:37:13 -0600
To: mom@abc.com
From: me@lotus.com

Dear Mom,

Thank you so much for your e-mail message. I was feeling
depressed and homesick, and I needed to hear the caring
words. Thanks for always knowing just what to say.

This Jewish proverb is so true: "God could not be everywhere
and therefore he made mothers."

Love,
Erica

E-mail Note #3

Subject: Final Essay
Date: Sun, 28 Jun 01:37:13 -0600
To: baker_lAsnu.edu
From: franco_p@snu.edu

Dear Dr. Baker,

Thank you for your comments on my final essay paper. You are correct, I could have put a little more time and effort into it.

Nevertheless, I thoroughly enjoyed your class, and although I had other things on my mind (like my looming graduation and job search), I did learn a great deal of practical information that I am certain will help me as I embark on life's adventures.

Thanks again, and wish me luck!

Sincerely,
Pattie Franco

The things taught in school are not an education but the means of an education.

Ralph Waldo Emerson

11

Summary

She always mentioned every flower in the arrangement or repeated the titles of books and their authors or the recordings and the soloists, almost as if she wanted to be certain that I understood that in her thanks she took as much care as I did in the selection.

Peter Rogers, in reference to Joan Crawford

Writing, any kind of writing, usually takes some time before the participant feels comfortable. If you are not familiar with writing thank-you notes, do not be alarmed if, initially, you feel like you are trying to ride a bike all over again. The pen may wobble a bit at first, and you might wish you had training wheels, but in time it will become second nature. By then, all of your friends and family will think you are the most hospitable and gracious person they know. And at that point, who is to say they are not right?

What you will find most appealing and satisfying about making thank-you notes a regular part of your life, is the impact you will be able to have on other people's lives. Taking the time to sit down and pen a short thought often means more to family, friends, and associates than a phone call.

This book is designed and written to illustrate the point that your wit, charm, and personality are the most important ingredients in any communication that you send. We have also included a few pointers on style and etiquette. Sending thank-you notes may seem like an obligatory gesture that is both burdensome and intimidating. But seen in a different light, thank-you notes can be a great deal more—the chance to express yourself fully, bring friends and family closer to you, and simply make someone feel good about themselves and what they have done.

Index